Smocking for Presents

Smocking for Presents

Kell Kelly and M. F. Deschenes

Webb&Bower

EXETER, ENGLAND

First published in Great Britain 1986 by
Webb & Bower (Publishers) Limited
9 Colleton Crescent, Exeter, Devon EX2 4BY

Edited, designed and illustrated by
E.T. Archive Ltd, 9 Chelsea Wharf, 15 Lots Road
London SW10 0QH

Designed by Julian Holland
Photography by Eileen Tweedy
Drawings and charts by Cedric Robson
Painted furniture lent by Dragons of Walton Street Ltd
Production by Nick Facer

British Library Cataloguing in Publication Data
Kelly, Kell
    Smocking for presents. — (Crafts for presents; 1)
    1. Smocking
    I. Title   II. Deschenes, Marie Françoise
    III. Series
    746.44   TT840

    ISBN 0-86350-090-0

Phototypeset by Tradespools Ltd, Frome, Somerset

Printed and bound in Hong Kong
by Mandarin Offset Marketing (HK) Ltd.

Contents

Introduction

Just what image does smocking bring to mind? Children's clothes? Throughout this book Marie Françoise and I will try and broaden this image. Smocking is a traditional craft, which has been brought out of the past and into the twentieth century. Modern pleating techniques and innovative design patterns have started a whole revolution in the way one thinks about this ancient craft.

We hope that the combination of ideas culled from new American designs and the French *chic* will inspire you while working these projects .

Background to smocking

Smocked garments can be traced back to as early as the sixth century AD but very little is known about this ancient peasant form of embroidery before the thirteenth century. The term 'to smock' evolved from the Anglo-Saxon word *smocc*. A *smocc* was traditionally an outer, loose-fitting garment, worn by peasants and English country gentlemen. The *smocc* protected the labourers' garments from becoming heavily soiled while they worked in the fields. Smocked garments were also worn by women, as a sort of undergarment, a camisole or *smicket* as it was called in the seventeenth century. Gradually this ancient form of decoration became more visible on women's outer clothes as well. By the nineteenth century, smocking was adorning the bodices of English and French ladies' fashions.

Today, smocking is having a fashion revival. In recent Paris collections Kenzo and Emmanuelle Kahn used smocking to adorn their creations. The lingerie departments of Dior and Lanvin in Paris contain many beautiful silk nightgowns embroidered with smocking. Fine clothing stores for children display smocked dresses in their front windows. Prince William's smocked suits are setting the trend in Paris—eagerly sought after by French customers.

In America, smocking has become a favourite pastime with the discovery of a manual pleating machine. It now takes only a few minutes to pleat rows of fabric. A whole industry has grown from re-interpreting traditional design patterns. Classical stitch patterns give way to romper suits smocked with Teddy bears, sailing boats, pony carts and more. Party clothes for little girls are exquisitely smocked with flower baskets, cherries, or bluebirds, with ribbons woven through the rows of pleats.

Best of all, smocking is no longer limited to children's clothes or pretty nightgowns. Every season suggests a project—Smocked Valentines, Easter eggs, and Christmas decorations. With a little bit of imagination there are many home decoration possibilities. So, when your children are grown up you will be able to smock beautiful pillows for your living room and bedrooms, not to mention all the gift items your friends will love to receive.

Basic supplies

Fabric
Smocking consists of many, many, pleats to give a soft, draped and full effect. So it is important to choose a top quality fabric which will hold the pleats and maintain a soft even line. Here is a list of 'fool-proof' fabrics for any beginner to use:

Quality cottons, such as light-weight poplins, Liberty-glazed cottons, designer-chintz (for home decoration projects), cotton flannels, cotton and polyester ' blends (45% cotton/55% polyester), wool and cotton or polyester blends, pure wools. Avoid pure synthetics and cheap bargain fabrics. If a pleater is used to prepare fabrics, avoid thick fabrics and pure wools, these need deeper pleats than the pleater can provide.

Amount of fabric
It is very difficult to say exactly how much fabric is needed, as this varies with the weight of a fabric and the elasticity of the smocking stitches used. But here are a few guidelines for beginners: for normal-weight fabrics, allow three times the width of fabric of the finished smocking; for light-weight fabrics, allow four times the width of the smocking.

Embroidery threads
Stranded embroidery cotton.
No 8 pearl cotton.
Rule of thumb: use three strands of embroidery cotton for cottons, four strands for wools. Use one strand of pearl cotton on wools. If silk is chosen, the project will need to be dry-cleaned.

Needles
No 8 crewel.

Pleating supplies—hand method
Deighton's transfer dots, 'K', are recommended for cottons; 'Q' for wools and fabrics that require a deeper pleat.
Heavy duty sewing thread, such as *Coats* quilting thread.
A steam iron.

Pleating with a pleater
There are several pleaters on the market today, but the easiest to use is the *Read* pleater.

There are several sizes available 'but the most practical and least expensive is the sixteen-row pleater. Investment in such a machine is highly recommended as it will save many hours of pleating by hand.

The only other supplies needed with a pleater are heavy-duty sewing thread and a steam iron.

Miscellaneous
Embroidery scissors, thimble, tailor's chalk and beeswax.

Preparing fabric for hand pleating

The first step to regular pleats is a straight fabric. The best method is to pull a thread from selvage to selvage in one straight line and then to cut along the line. The fabric should be straight and square.

Cut the dot transfer to two rows more than the desired numbers of rows to be smocked. Place the transfer face down on the wrong side of the fabric and secure with basting stitches. With a low temperature iron, press down firmly; do not rub the transfer with the iron. Do not use a hot iron—this will make the dots indelible.

Once the dots are transferred on to the fabric, start picking them up to form pleats. With a thread 16 cm (6 in) longer than the width of the fabric, knotted at one end and in a contrasting colour, begin picking up the dots from right to left as shown in the diagram.

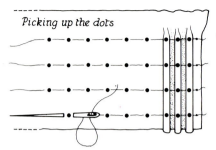

Picking up the dots

If the fabric is dark, and it is difficult to see the dots, the transfer can be used in another way. Baste it down securely so it does not move and pick up the dots by sewing through the paper, then tearing it away when you have finished.

N.B. The above method is a better way to pick up dots if they are difficult to wash out or if they are difficult to see.

Slowly pull the gathering threads together to form the pleats. To make the pleats sit correctly gently pull the fabric from top to bottom. When all the pleats are in place, set with a steam iron.

On one side of the fabric, begin tying off the gathering threads, in pairs with an overhand knot. All the knots should be in a straight line. Now, run your nails over the pleats to divide them evenly. The pleated fabric should be 3.5 cm (1¼ in) narrower than the required size. Tie off the opposite side, respecting the vertical line again. This step of evenly dividing the pleats is very important as they form the final structure for the embroidery.

Preparing fabric for a machine pleater

1) Straighten fabric.
2) Thread needles on pleater.
3) Roll fabric on to a dowel stick or a magnetic feed rod.
4) Run the fabric through pleater.
5) Now follow the same instructions as for hand pleating.

Smocking's golden rules

1) Never smock the first and last three full pleats as these will become the seam allowance.

2) To start a smocking thread firmly knot one end of the embroidery cotton, preferably the cut end from the skein. On the wrong side of the fabric, pick up the top of the fourth pleat and come through to the right side, on left side of pleat.

3) To end a thread, go to the wrong side of the fabric on the right side of the pleat. Make a back stitch and tie off thread with an overhand knot.

4) Pick up only one-third of the pleat. If you pick up more you reduce elasticity.

5) Keep needle parallel to gathering threads.

6) Make sure embroidery cotton lies flat; running floss through beeswax will help.

7) Use blunt end of needle to rip out a mistake.

8) In the areas where there is no smocking and where the stitch will be too elastic to retain its shape, you will need to back-smock on wrong side of fabric using a cable stitch.

9) Block all smocking before mounting. Pin piece to ironing board, making sure it is straight. Steam the piece (the iron should not touch the smocking) and let dry.

For all the projects in this book, the fabric must be prepared for smocking. Whether you choose to pleat by hand or with a pleater, follow the instructions already given. General measurements and the number of rows to smock are given, but will need to be adapted to your size and materials.

N.B. For all projects the pleat spacing is the standard 8 mm (¼ in) or 1 cm (⅓ in) space.

Basic beginner stitches

The following stitches are worked from left to right.

For left-handed stitchers: to adapt stitch diagrams, turn them upside down. Hold the work vertically, working down, rather than across.

N.B. For clarity, the needle has been drawn at an angle in some of these diagrams. Remember always to keep the needle parallel to the gathering thread.

Outline stitch
Pick up a pleat just above the gathering thread keeping embroidery cotton above the needle.

Stem stitch
Work this the same as outline, BUT keep embroidery cotton below needle.

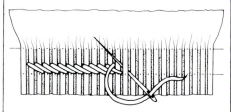

Wheat stitch
This stitch is formed by combining one row of outline and, directly underneath it, one row of stem.

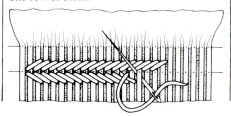

Cable stitch
This is the most important stitch a beginner can learn, and is one of the easiest. It is used to 'picture smock'. Pick up a pleat with embroidery cotton above the needle (up cable), pick up the next pleat with embroidery cotton below the needle (down cable). Continue the row, keeping tension even.

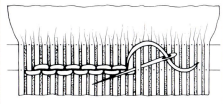

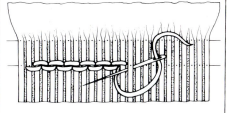

N.B. These first four stitches are not very elastic. When starting a project, smock the first row with one of these stitches, unless otherwise indicated.

Baby Wave stitch
Stitch a down cable, keeping embroidery cotton below needle, pick up the next pleat half-way to the next gathering thread, stitch an up cable keeping embroidery cotton above needle. Continue the row in this manner.

For diagram see Diamond stitch.

Full Wave stitch
Stitch as for baby wave, but using full space between gathering threads.

Diamond stitch

A diamond shape is formed when two consecutive rows of baby wave are stitched together. If the first row begins with a down cable, the second row would begin with an up cable.

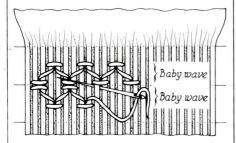

Diamond stitch variation

Stitch as for diamond, but use three cables instead of one.

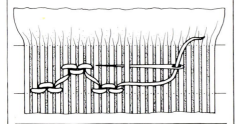

Crossed Diamond stitch

Starting row with a down cable, stitch one row of full wave. With a contrasting colour of embroidery cotton on the same row, but on the top gathering thread, start with an up cable, crossing down with a full space wave.

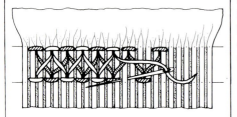

Wheat and Diamond stitch combination

Stitch six outline stitches, one baby wave, six outline stitches, one baby wave, six outline stitches, one baby wave. On the second row, directly under outline stitch, stitch six stem, one baby wave, six stem, one baby wave and so on.

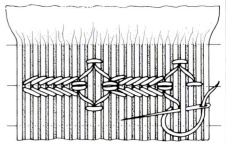

Crossed Diamond stitch variation

Stitch as for a crossed diamond, but using three cables instead of one.

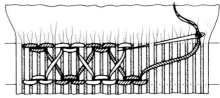

Several projects in this book can be made with these first ten stitches. The bolster was stitched entirely with a crossed diamond pattern, and the baby bonnet uses the diamond variation. A party dress for a little girl could also be made using the baby wave to stitch the front bodice of the dress, but remember to stitch the first row with a stem or cable stitch.

Intermediate level stitches

Trellis stitch

The trellis stitch is a combination of cable, stem and outline stitch and needs practice to obtain even spacing.

Remember—when going up, embroidery cotton stays down; when going down, embroidery cotton stays up.

Divide the space between the gathering threads into four by eye. On the bottom gathering thread, stitch a down cable, then, working upwards, work a stem stitch, keeping the embroidery cotton below the needle, on each of the next four pleats, a quarter the way up, half-way up, three-quarters the way up, and the whole way up until the top of the gathering thread is reached. Then stitch an up cable. Go down the step ladder in the same fashion, but using an outline stitch and keeping embroidery cotton above needle. Continue row in this manner. Remember to keep needle parallel to the stitches opposite.

The trellis can be stitched in various heights. Combining the baby wave with a full space trellis will give a heart-shaped pattern. This stitch has a number of interesting design patterns, once the basics have been mastered.

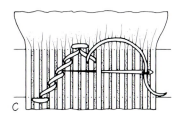

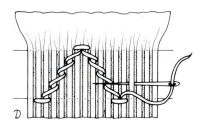

Surface Honeycomb stitch

This stitch is worked in a similar way to the baby wave, the difference being that the same pleat is used twice. Stitch a down cable; half-way up to the next gathering thread, pick up the same pleat; stitch an up cable; going down, pick up the same pleat half-way down and stitch a down cable. Continue row in this manner.

Several rows of this stitch are less elastic than the baby wave.

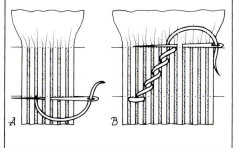

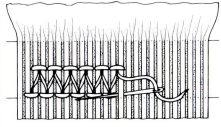

Honeycomb stitch

This is a very elastic stitch, so an entire project worked with it needs less fabric. (Two and a half times the amount of fabric instead of three).

Start stitch with a down cable, but bring the needle back through both pleats (A). Insert the needle back into valley of the right side of second pleat, bring it back through to right side of the fabric in valley of first pleat on top gathering thread (B). Stitch a cable through both pleats (C). Insert needle through valley of third pleat coming up through valley of second pleat on bottom gathering thread, stitch a cable coming through both fourth and third pleat (D). Continue row (E).

N.B. The following two stitches are worked from right to left.

Simple Van Dyke stitch

Bring the needle to the right side of fabric on left side of pleat, stitch a down cable through two pleats. Move up to next gathering thread, pick up same pleat as well as next one. Stitch an up cable coming through both pleats and moving down, pick up same pleat and the following one. Stitch a down cable through two pleats. Continue row in this manner. The simple Van Dyke may be worked at half-space intervals between the gathering threads and full-space intervals.

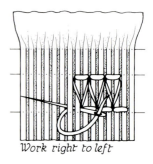

Work right to left

Double Van Dyke stitch

Work this stitch as for the simple Van Dyke, over half-space intervals, but move upwards four to six times, before moving down. This forms a zigzag pattern.

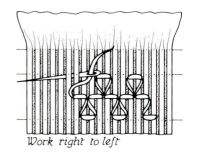

Work right to left

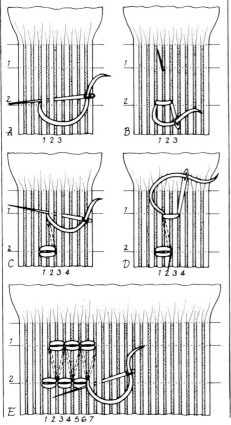

Advanced and decorative stitches

Picture smocking with Stacked Cables

By stacking consecutive rows of uneven cable stitches, a myriad of designs can be created. The technique is not difficult, but the regularity that should be obtained for successful picture smocking is. Only hours of practice will accomplish this. Start learning how to stack cables by building simple pyramids. Work a base row of seven cables, starting with a down cable (A). On the last cable, bring the needle to the wrong side of fabric, turning fabric upside down. One pleat over to the right, pick up a down cable, work five cables (B). Turn fabric around, one pleat over, stitch three cables, turn over, stitch one cable. The pyramid is now complete (C).

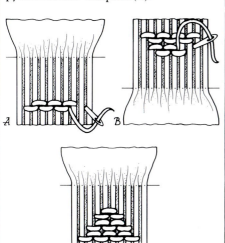

Cable Flowerette

Start with a down cable (A), stitch three cables (B), on the third cable, keeping embroidery cotton above needle, turn fabric over and finish flower with an up cable (C).

Use these flowers to adorn a row of baby wave.

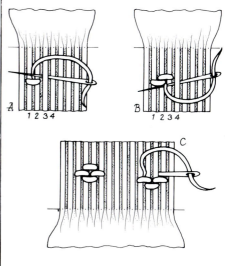

Double Flowerette

Work three cables, beginning with a down cable. With the last cable, bring needle through all four pleats, making sure the needle comes out directly below first cable stitch (A). Work three cables, beginning with an up cable (B). End flower securing it on the wrong side with a back stitch and overhand knot.

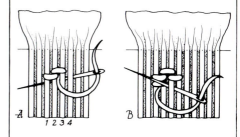

Bar stitch

This is a very easy stitch to do; it is often used in picture smocking as well as in geometric patterns to join two peaks with a contrasting colour. It can be worked over two, three or four pleats. It is simply several down cables worked one on top of the other. Work as many needed to fill space. End stitch with an overhand knot.

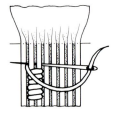

French Knot

Bring needle to right side of fabric at *top* of pleat. Wind floss around needle two, three, or four times. Bring needle to wrong side of fabric close to where it started. Holding embroidery cotton on needle, glide needle through to wrong side of fabric. Secure cotton in the usual manner.

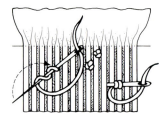

Chain stitch

Leaves as well as flowers can be made with this classic embroidery stitch. Bring needle to right side of fabric at the *top* of pleat, rather than the *side*. Bring needle back through same pleat close to where it first emerged and push it through two pleats coming out at the *top* of pleat, catching embroidery cotton under needle to form loop (A). Bring needle to wrong side of fabric on *side* of pleat (B). Secure with overhand knot on wrong side of fabric.

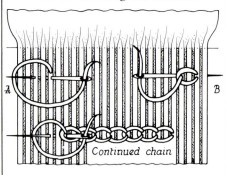

Bouillon Rose

Bring needle to right side of fabric at *top* of pleat, push needle through *top* of two or three pleats depending on the size and shape of the rose; do not pull the needle all the way out (A). Wind floss around needle, as many times as needed to fill space and, holding floss lightly, pull needle through (B). Arrange and secure as for bouillon knot. Work three to form a rose, adding a few chain stitches to form leaves.

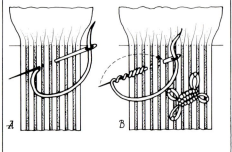

Bouillon Knot

Bring needle to *top* of pleat coming back through *top* of pleat at position 2 (A). Come back to right side of fabric at position 1, bringing needle out only half-way (B). Wind embroidery cotton around needle enough times to fill space between positions 1 and 2 (C). Holding cotton on needle, gently glide needle through (D). Bring needle to wrong side of fabric at position 2 (E). Arrange bouillon knot with blunt end of needle pulling gently in place (F). Secure to fabric in usual manner.

Bouillon Knot Loop stitch

Bring needle to right side of fabric at *top* of pleat, push needle back through same pleat just above starting position but as with the other knots, push the needle half-way through the pleat (A). Wind embroidery cotton around needle twenty times and, holding cotton lightly, glide needle through pleat to form loop (B). Bring needle to wrong side of fabric at entry position. Arrange loop with a tacking stitch around bouillon rose (C). Do several to surround flower.

These *Bouillon Knot Loop* stitches need a great deal of practice to do well, so do not be too discouraged if your first knots are not well done.

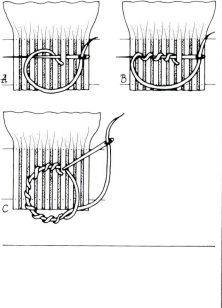

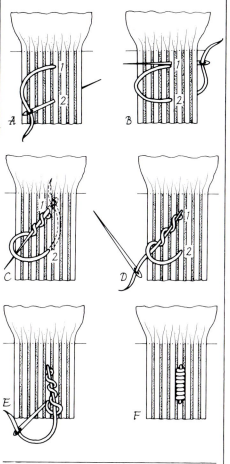

Curtain tie back

Here is one of the easiest, original, least expensive and versatile projects in this book—a smocked satin ribbon which could be used as a curtain tie back. Or perhaps there is a wedding in sight? 'Something borrowed, something blue . . .' A smocked satin garter for the bride would be a beautiful souvenir.

Materials

satin ribbon—1.5 m (1½ yd) 6 or 8 cm (2¼ or 3 in) wide
embroidery cotton—2 colour design

2 brass rings, 3 or 4 cm (1 or 1½ in) in diameter
1 dot transfer sheet for hand pleating

Pleating and stitch instructions
Stitch narrow hem on each end of ribbon.
Pleat four rows.
The stitches used for this project are:
cable and *trellis*.
Follow stitch diagram to smock.

Finishing
Remove all the gathering threads.
Sew brass rings to each end of ribbon.

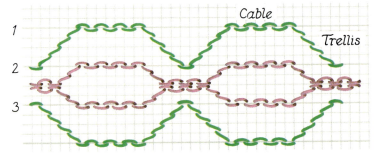

Smocked trimmed basket

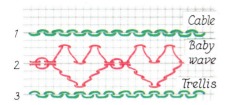

1   *Cable*

2   *Baby wave*

3   *Trellis*

Here is a project that is very adaptable. A perfect accessory for the nursery, or a woman's dressing table; an attractive way to decorate a sewing basket or adorn a baby's crib. This trimmed basket would be a double treat at Easter. And why not decorate a Christmas fruit basket with a smocked red and green ruffle?

Depending on the size of the basket, this project is quick and easy to do. There are only three rows of smocking.

Materials
a basket
strips of cotton fabric. Measure the top
   diameter of the basket, multiply by three.
The height of the strips depends on the basket and personal taste. Allow 3 cm (1 in) more for hems.
embroidery cotton—2 skeins
1 dot transfer sheet for hand pleating

General instructions
The basket shown needed two strips of fabric, 12 × 90 cm (4½ × 35 in). Pin strips together, and stitch along seam line. Press seam open. Machine stitch narrow hem, top and bottom. Pleat four rows directly underneath top hem. Prepare and divide pleats.

The following stitches are used:
cable, *baby wave* and *trellis*.
Follow stitch diagram to smock.

Finishing
Remove all gathering threads. Block. Matching up smocking, right sides together, pin side seams, stitch along seam line. Attach ruffle to basket in several places with tacking stitches.

Smocked collar

This pretty collar is a perfect gift item to give at any occasion. It can be worn to dress up a round-neck shirt or sweater, for a child or an adult.

Materials
ready made cotton ruffle. To determine length
  of ruffle, multiply neck measurements by four.
embroidery cotton—1 skein per colour
bias binding
1 pearl button
1 dot transfer sheet for hand pleating

Pleating and stitch instructions
Pleat six rows.
Place the ruffle on a table, and start dividing the pleats so they form a circle. The first two rows of threads will be pulled tighter than the last four rows which will fan out. Steam the circle of pleats to set them in place.
The stitches used in this design are: *cable* and *trellis*.
Follow the stitch diagram to smock; the tension should be tighter on the top rows and looser on the bottom rows.

Finishing
Remove all but the first row of gathering threads. This first gathering thread prevents the collar from pulling out of shape. Pin down the bias tape, right sides together, stitch close to smocking. Turn tape over and slip stitch to back side of collar. Sew on pearl button, make a bouillon stitch loop buttonhole.

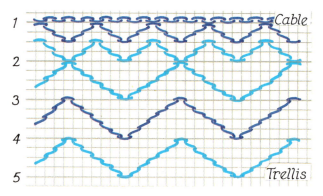

Smocked bonnet

This is an easy project for a beginner to make and on which to practise stitches at the same time.

Materials

suggested fabrics—cotton poplin, fine swiss
  baptiste—110 × 32 cm (41 × 12 in)
bias binding
eyelet ruffle trim
satin ribbon—1 strip 50 × 0.5 cm (19 × $\frac{1}{4}$ in)
  2 strips 1.5 × 30 cm ($\frac{1}{2}$ × 11$\frac{1}{2}$ in)
embroidery cotton—4 colour design
1 dot transfer sheet for hand pleating

Cutting instructions

Fold fabric in half, make a mark 30 cm (11$\frac{1}{2}$ in) high on fold line, and 15 cm (5$\frac{1}{2}$ in) high on selvage. Draw diagonal line between the two marks. Cut on this line. Machine stitch narrow hem, on straight edge. Stitch ruffle to hemmed edge. On unhemmed edge, run a basting stitch, along seam line.

Pleating and stitch instructions

Pleat six rows directly underneath hem. Prepare and divide pleats. The stitches used for this project are: *wheat, diamond variation, french knot*. Follow stitch diagram to smock.

Finishing

Remove gathering threads. Block. Draw up basting stitch so edge measures 15 cm (5$\frac{1}{2}$ in). Stitch on bias tape. Insert thin satin ribbon, through bias tape. Tie with a bow. Stitch satin ribbons to each side at top of smocked edge.

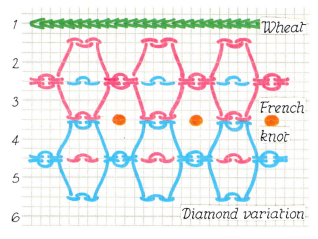

Wheat

French knot

Diamond variation

Smocked heart pincushion

Here is a charming and practical way to have scissors, pins and needles at hand. This is a perfect little gift—easy and inexpensive to make, the pincushion can take on many shapes: heart, Christmas tree, apple, whatever takes one's fancy.

Materials

cotton fabric—15 × 50 cm (5½ × 19 in) for smocking
fabric for backing—14 cm (5 in) square
gros grain ribbon—1 m (39 in)
silk cord—50 cm (19 in)
1 pair folding scissors
embroidery cotton—1 skein
1 dot transfer sheet for hand pleating

Pleating and stitch instructions

Pleat fourteen rows. Prepare and divide pleats.
The stitches used in this project are: *stacked cables* and *cable* for backsmocking.
Follow stitch diagram to smock.

Finishing

Remove gathering threads, and block.
Cut out cardboard heart pattern. This one measured 12 cm (4½ in) square. Remember to allow for seam allowance.
Mark pattern on wrong side of smocked piece with tailor's chalk.
With small machine stitches, stitch along pattern line. This will prevent fraying. Trim just outside this line of stitching.
Pin fabric back to smocked heart, right sides together, baste in place. Trim square to shape of heart.
Machine stitch on seam line, leaving small opening on side for stuffing.
Trim and clip seams, turn to right side. Stuff, slip stitch opening.
Pin silk cord in place, placing end at top centre of heart and tack.
Pin gros grain ribbon to back top centre, in this way hiding silk cord ends. Hand stitch gros grain ribbon in place.
Stitch other end of ribbon to scissors.

Stacked cable

Smocked sampler alphabet

Alphabet samplers are quite popular today, whether they are old collector's items or newly stitched ones for friends. This smocked alphabet would be a welcome and original addition to any collection. With just a little imagination, the idea can be adapted to a christening or wedding sampler as well. A gift idea that will be cherished throughout a lifetime. It is not a difficult project, but one must know how to 'picture smock' in order to decorate the sampler. It is also economical—we used leftover embroidery cotton to smock the flowers. So do not throw away your bits and pieces, but save them for this project, an enchanting sampler.

Materials

fabric—26 × 90 cm (10 × 35 in)
embroidery cotton—2 skeins for dominant colours
leftover embroidery cotton for flowers
1 ready made frame
2 dot transfer sheets for hand pleating

Pleating and stitch instructions

Pleat twenty-five rows. Prepare and divide pleats.
The stitches used for this project are:
cable, stacked cables, trellis, stem, bar, chain, double flowerette, full wave.
Follow stitch diagram to smock.

Finishing

Remove all gathering threads and block straight.
Frame sampler in the ready made frame.

E F G H

I N O P

U U U W *Bar*

Z

Double flowerette

Full wave

Chain

Stacked cable

Stem and cable

Trellis

Smocking for the bedroom

The first of our co-ordinated bedroom projects is a smocked negligé. We have chosen a lovely cotton crêpe fabric for each project.

This nightgown is for special occasions—a wonderful gift for a special friend. Greeting the one you love in such a pretty, feminine, romantic gown, will certainly not go unnoticed.

The smocked bolster is the second project. There is very little smocking involved and the sewing up is not difficult. This attractive covering for pillows adds a very feminine touch to a bedroom or living room decoration scheme. An easy and impressive project, and a beautiful gift for a stitcher at any level.

The third bedroom project is a smocked lampshade. It could be co-ordinated with your curtain material—it would be lovely smocked in chintz. This is another project where the sewing up is easy to do.

Smocked negligé

Materials

2 lengths of cotton crêpe fabric
2 ribbons, 6 cm × 1 m (2¼ × 39 in) and 2
  ribbons 1 × 50 cm (⅓ × 19 in)
embroidery cotton—2 skeins per colour
2 dot transfer sheets for hand pleating

Pleating and stitch instructions

Bodice
Machine stitch narrow top hem, front and
back.
Pleat thirteen rows front and back, directly
underneath hem.
Waistline
Front only, 2 cm (⅔ in) above waistline,
pleat seven rows.
Prepare and divide pleats.

The stitches used in this project are:
cable, *trellis*, and *bouillon knot*.
Backsmocking is used on rows three and
four at the waist.
Follow stitch diagram to smock.
To smock the back of the negligé bodice,
follow rows one through twelve, leaving
out the *bouillon knot* stitches.
The back waist is not smocked.

Finishing

Remove all gathering threads. Block.
Pin wide ribbon to waistline smocking
(right sides together), baste in place.
Pin front to back, matching up smocking,
stitch along seam allowance. Press open
seams.
Pin ribbon straps in place and stitch in
place.
Machine stitch bottom hem.

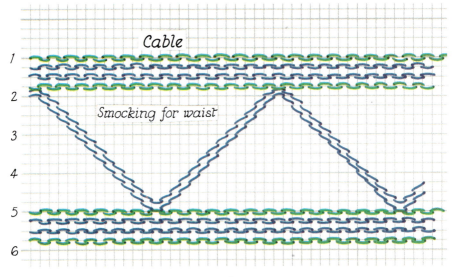

Front and back, bodice

Cable

Trellis

Bouillon knot

1
2
3
4
5
6
7
8
9
10

Smocked bolster

Materials

1 bolster pillow, 40 cm long × 46 cm (15 × 17½ in) round
large width cotton crêpe or chintz fabric—
   2 strips cut 10 × 120 cm (4 × 47¼ in) (A)
   2 strips 12 × 46 cm (4½ × 17½ in) (B)
   1 band 35 × 46 cm (13¼ × 17½ in) (C)
embroidery cotton—2 colour design
satin ribbon—1 m (39 in)
1 dot transfer sheet for hand pleating

Pleating and stitch instructions

Machine stitch narrow hem on strips (A)
Pleat five rows on unhemmed edge.
Prepare and divide pleats.
The only stitch used in this project is:
three cable *crossed diamond*.
Follow stitch diagram to smock.

Finishing

Remove gathering threads. With right sides together, pin smocked strips to sides of wide band (C) (strips pinned on 46 cm [17½ in] side).

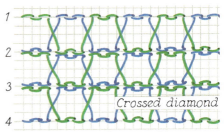

Crossed diamond

Stitch in place just above smocking.
Machine stitch casing for ribbon on each of the remaining strips. With right sides facing down, place strips on top of smocked strips, pin and stitch on same stitch line as smocked strips.
Stitch close the smocked strips with a french seam, matching up all the rows of smocking.
With right sides together, pin sides together and stitch along seam line, keeping smocked ruffle clear.
Cut ribbon in half, insert into casing, tie with a bow, put pillow in case, insert other ribbon into casing, close with a bow.

Smocked lampshade

Materials
a wire frame lampshade
fabric—three times top diameter
embroidery cotton—2 skeins
1 dot transfer sheet for hand pleating

Pleating and stitch instructions
Machine stitch narrow top hem.
Pleat nine rows, directly underneath hem.
Prepare and divide pleats as on page 18.

The stitches used for this project are:
cable, *baby wave* and *trellis*.
Follow stitch diagram to smock.

Finishing
Remove all but the first gathering thread.
Block. With right sides together, matching up smocking, pin side seams. Stitch.
Stitch bottom hem 2 cm ($\frac{2}{3}$ in) longer than frame. Attach to top with tacking stitches.

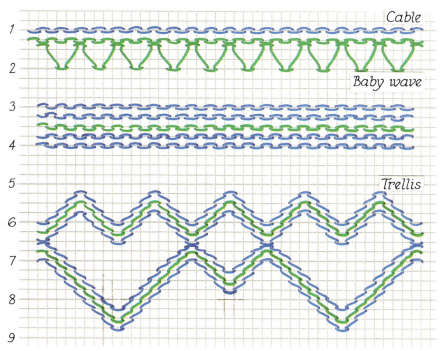

Smocked skirt

This smocked evening skirt will be the envy of your next dinner party. An intermediate stitcher can create it with little trouble. The sewing up involves no more than sewing two side seams, putting on a waistband, and a zipper. Although the front and back both have twenty-three rows of smocking, the Bargello inspired design, interpreted with the *Van Dyke* stitch is worked much more quickly than one would expect. The natural elasticity of smocking hugs the hips and the fullness of the fabric flares out to give a very sophisticated look.

Materials

fabric—soft fabrics such as wool and cotton blends—three times the width of waist. Finished length is hemmed at the calf.
zipper, skirt hook and eye
embroidery cotton or silk—2 skeins of each colour
4 dot transfer sheets for hand pleating
commercial skirt pattern

Pleating and stitch instructions

Pleat twenty-four rows (front and back). Prepare and divide pleats 3 cm (1 in) less than the width of waist.
The only stitch used in this design is: *double Van Dyke*
Start the design on the fifth gathering thread in the darkest colour.
Remember the *Van Dyke* is worked from right to left. When working rows above, i.e., four to one, knot each thread when arriving at top gathering thread and start in the next row with new thread. This will ensure that the smocking retains its elasticity.
Follow stitch diagram to smock.

Finishing

Remove all but the first gathering thread; this first thread holds the waistline in place.
Using a standard commercial skirt pattern, sew according to directions, remembering to match up the rows of smocking.

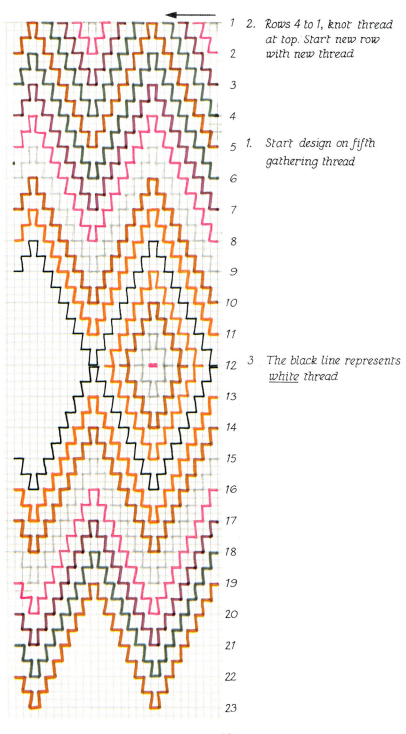

1   2. Rows 4 to 1, knot thread
2   at top. Start new row
        with new thread
3

4

5   1. Start design on fifth
        gathering thread
6

7

8

9

10

11

12   3 The black line represents
       <u>white</u> thread
13

14

15

16

17

18

19

20

21

22

23

33

Smocked baby's blouse

Here is a very pretty blouse to make for a baby. It is a perfect christening gift, and, believe it or not, this blouse takes very little time to make and involves practically no sewing up.

What is the secret? This is an inexpensive plain round-neck, button-down-the-back blouse bought in a department store and the neckline has been transformed. The result is this pretty smocked blouse which involved little work. Baby's wardrobe will certainly flourish with such an easy and inexpensive project.

Materials
a plain round-neck blouse
fabric (matching or co-ordinated)—a strip 8 cm (3 in) high and three times the diameter of neckline
embroidery cotton—2 colour design
bias binding
1 dot transfer for hand pleating

Pleating and stitch instructions
Machine stitch a narrow bottom hem.
Pleat five rows.
Prepare and divide pleats following the directions for the 'Smocked Collar'.
The stitches used in this design are:
cable, trellis, chain, french knot, and *stacked cable.*
Follow the stitch diagram to smock. Remember the tension should be tighter on the top row of smocking.

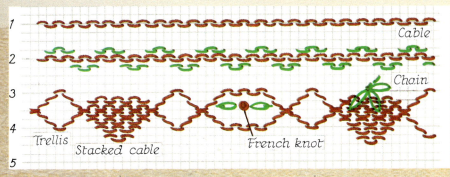

Finishing

Finish this project in the same way as the collar, excluding sewing on of pearl button and making of buttonhole.

Smocked evening bag

Many French couturiers design accessories to add that special ingredient to their collection. This stunning smocked evening bag will add just that right ingredient to an evening ensemble. It makes a superb present for a special friend.

Materials

suggested fabrics: moiré, heavy taffeta, satin
brocade—40 cm × 1 m (15 × 39 in)
pearl cotton—3 skeins per colour
10 brass rings, 1 cm ($\frac{1}{3}$ in) round
1 heavy silk cord 120 cm (45 in) long
1 dot transfer sheet for hand pleating

Pleating and stitch instructions

Slip stitch a 3 cm (1 in) top hem.
Machine stitch narrow bottom hem.
Directly underneath top hem, pleat twelve rows.
Directly underneath bottom hem, pleat seven rows.
Prepare and divide pleats.
The only stitch used in this design is:
trellis.
Follow stitch diagram to smock.

Finishing

Remove only the first top twelve gathering threads.
On bottom smocking remove gathering threads where there is smocking.
In line with each bottom point in the zig-zag design, from top smocking to bottom smocking, take in 2 cm ($\frac{2}{3}$ in) wide darts. (This is done on wrong side of fabric.)
On the right side of fabric, using a whipping stitch, alternating colours of pearl cotton, embroider each dart seam.
With right sides together, pin side seams, matching up smocking, stitch along seam. Try and keep bottom gathering threads clear.
Make a braided tassel, knot both ends. Pull bottom gathering threads as tight as possible. Push tassel through small hole.

Tie off gathering threads. Secure tassel in place with small tacking stitches, closing small hole at same time.
Make a thin braid 60 cm (23 in) long with pearl cotton; do not knot ends.
Stitch rings on at top of each point.
Insert braid into rings, knot each end.
Secure satin cord to interior of bag with tacking stitches.

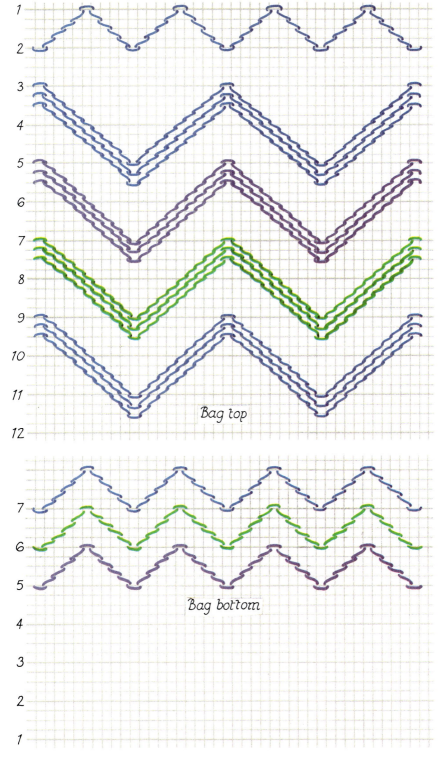

Bag top

Bag bottom

Sampler pincushion

Here is a pretty way for beginners to practise their newly learned stitches. This small ruffle-trimmed pincushion is not only pretty but useful too. Put it on baby's dressing table or use it as a tiny pillow for baby to hold. This cushion is quick to do, and can be made in no time as a small gift. After this design has been mastered, it can be changed by stitching other designs in place of the balloons.

Materials
plain cotton fabric—18 × 75 cm (7 × 29 in)
printed fabric for backing and ruffle
embroidery cotton—5 colour design
1 dot transfer sheet for hand pleating
synthetic stuffing

Pleating and stitch instructions
Pleat seventeen rows. Prepare and divide pleats.
The stitches used in this sampler are:
baby wave, crossed diamond, cable and *baby wave combination, cable* and *trellis combination, cable, trellis (half-space* and *full), surface honeycomb, honeycomb, stacked cables, outline* and *stem.*
Follow stitch diagram to smock. Backsmock in the area where there is no stitching (see page 7).

Finishing
Remove all gathering threads. Block.
Iron open seam allowance.
Cut a 3 cm (1 in) strip of printed fabric to form ruffle. Run two rows of basting stitches along one edge of ruffle. Pin to smocked piece, drawing in basting threads to adjust size. Stitch along seam line.
Cut square of fabric for back, right sides together, pin to smocked piece. Stitch along seam line, leaving small opening. Trim seams. Turn to right side. Stuff, close with slip stitch.

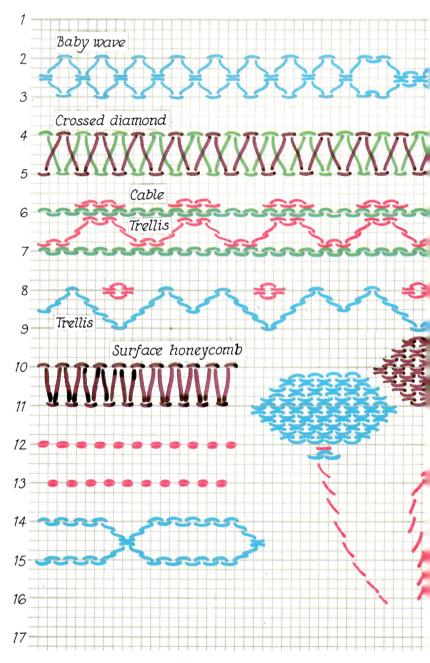

Baby wave

Crossed diamond

Cable

Trellis

Trellis

Surface honeycomb

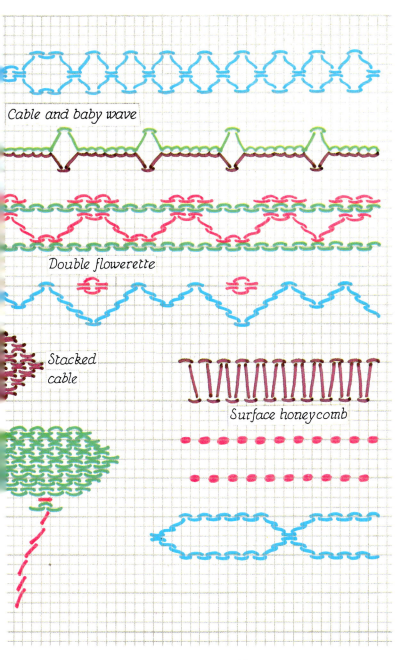

Cable and baby wave

Double flowerette

Stacked
cable

Surface honeycomb

Picture smocking sampler pillow

What child would not cherish this animal zoo pillow, complete with royal guardsman? I am sure that all your family will encourage you when they see this enchanting project—an ideal way to try out picture smocking. Why throw away sample work? Here is a better solution. While learning to stack cables evenly, you will be creating an animal zoo to delight children and yourself.

Pleating and stitch instruction
Pleat sixteen rows. Prepare and divide pleats.
Most of the stitches used on this sampler are *stacked cables*. Accent stitches used to complement the design pattern are: *bar, chain, french knot, stem, crossed diamond*. For further reference, read section on 'picture smocking'.

Materials
plain cotton fabric—25 × 90 cm (9½ × 35 in)
fabric square for backing
110 cm (42 in) satin ribbon
broderie anglaise—1 m (39 in)
embroidery cotton, multicoloured, use leftovers
synthetic stuffing

To smock an animal sampler, use the following diagram as a guide, placing as many ducks, rabbits, etc., as wished. Use the diagram on pages 22–3 to stitch the child's name.

Finishing
Remove all gathering threads. Block. Frame the sampler with four strips of satin ribbon. Pin four strips to front of sampler. Stitch in place. Trim excess fabric.

Run two rows of tacking stitches along one edge of broderie anglaise. Pin to smocked piece, drawing in tacking to adjust size.

With right sides together, pin fabric backing to sampler and stitch in place leaving small opening. Clip corners, turn to right side. Stuff. Close opening with slip stitch.

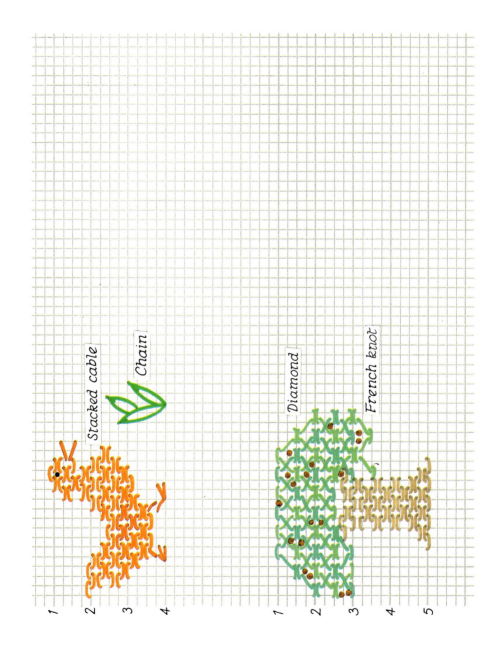

Stacked cable

Chain

Diamond

French knot

Bar

Stem

Smocked mobile

This project is for advanced-level stitchers, as it involves 'picture smocking'

Materials
4 polystyrene balls—23 cm (8⅔ in) round
cotton fabric—4 strips cut 75 cm (29 in) long,
   and exact height of ball
satin ribbon—4 m (4 yd)
2 wooden sticks for crossbar
embroidery cotton—1 skein per colour
2 dot transfer sheets for hand pleating

Pleating and stitch instructions
Pleat as many rows as the height of the ball, i.e., for an 11 cm (4¼ in) ball, pleat 10 rows. Prepare and divide pleats.
The stitches used in this project are:
Ducks—*cable, stacked cables, trellis, chain, french knot.*
Birds—*stem, stacked cables, french knot, chain.*
Train—*cable, stacked cable, stem trellis, french knot, bar.*
Cowboy and Indian—*cable, stacked cables, trellis, outline, chain, bar.*
Each ball was finished using the *whipped spider web stitch.*
Follow stitch diagrams to smock, centering each design according to size of ball.

Finishing
Remove all but the first and last gathering thread. Block. With right sides together, matching up smocking, pin side seams, stitch. Press seam open (A).
Insert ball. Pull gathering threads tight, to enclose ball. Tie off threads. If edges of fabric overlap, trim. Sew long tacking stitches over raw edges of fabric so that they lie flat (B).
Hide these raw edges with a 'whipped spider web stitch' (C).
Make a rosette ribbon with loop and attach to top of each ball. Balance balls on crossbars and glue in place. Tie another ribbon to crossbar to hang over crib.

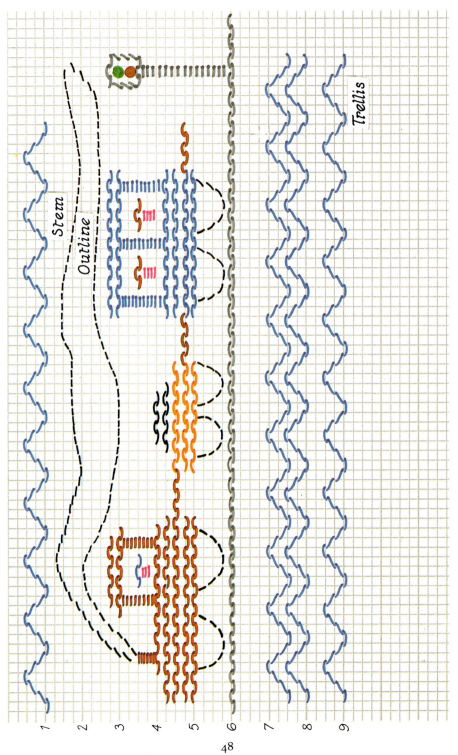

Stem

Outline

Trellis

48

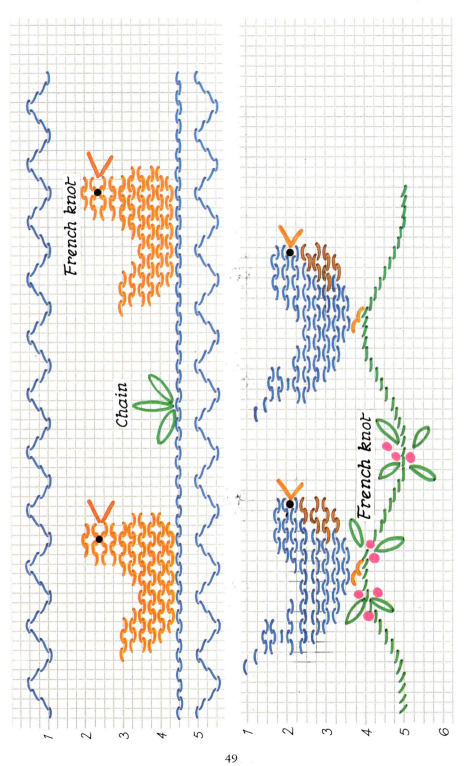

French knot

Chain

French knot

49

Bouillon knot

Chain

Trellis

1
2
3
4
5
6
7

Finishing the mobile

Pin side seams together and stitch (1).
Insert ball. Pull gathering threads tight
and tack over raw edges (2).
Hide edges with a 'whipped spider web'
stitch (3) and (4).
Make a rosette ribbon with loop and attach
to top of each ball (5).

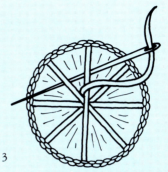

3

Work a Whipped Spider Web
over the raw edges

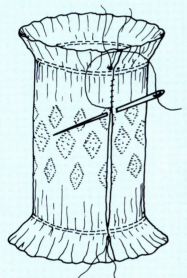

1

Pin sides together and stitch

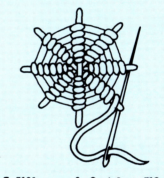

4

A Whipped Spider Web

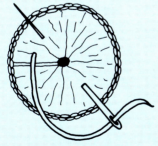

2

Tack over raw edges

5

Christening sampler smocked ball

Why not stitch a christening sampler in smocking as a change from cross stitch or needlepoint. The principle for this project is the same as for the smocked mobile but the ball is larger.

Materials

1 polystyrene ball—32 cm (12¼ in) round
1 strip cotton fabric—16 × 90 cm (6 × 35 in)
embroidery cotton—4 colour design
satin ribbon—1.5 m (1½ yd)
1 dot transfer sheet for hand pleating

General instructions

Follow instructions for smocked mobile, except crossbars.

Stitch instructions

The stitches used in this project are:
baby wave, stacked cable, trellis, bar, stem, full wave, double flowerette.
Follow stitch diagram, using diagram for alphabet on pages 22–3 to do lettering.

Finishing

Finish ball as for mobile.

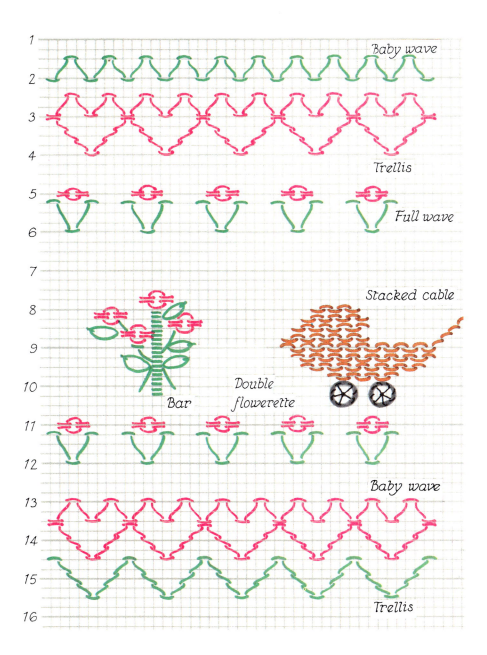

Baby wave

Trellis

Full wave

Stacked cable

Bar

Double
flowerette

Baby wave

Trellis

53

'Kiss the Cook'

An ideal gift for the keen cook.

Materials
gingham fabric—
    skirt: 80 × 115 cm (31½ × 44 in)
    waistband: 10 × 200 cm (4 × 76 in)
    1 strip—10 × 100 cm (4 × 39 in) (A),
    2 strips—10× 24 cm (4 × 9 in) (B)
smocked bib: plain cotton fabric—
    20 × 70 cm (7½ × 26½ in)
velcro—25 cm (9½ in)
embroidery cotton—5 colour design
1 dot transfer sheet for hand smocking

Pleating and stitch instructions
Pleat eighteen rows.
Prepare and divide pleats.
The stitches used in this project are: *stacked cables*, *stem* and *outline*. Follow stitch diagram to smock (count pleats to centre design).

Finishing
Skirt
On top edge of skirt, machine stitch two rows of basting stitches from selvage to selvage.
Draw basting edge up to 52 cm (19½ in). Mark centre. Mark centre of waistband strip, turn in 5 mm (¼ in) hem on each edge. Baste in place. With right sides together, pin waistband to skirt, matching centre marks. Machine stitch in place. Trim seams. Turn waistband to wrong side, pin to skirt. Machine stitch continuing along the waistband tie strip. Hem ends of waistband. Slip stitch bottom hem.
Smocked Bib
Remove gathering threads and block.
On top and bottom of bib, sew on the two strips (B) treating as seam binding. Apply strip (A) to sides of bib, pin one end to each side, thus forming loop to go over head. Machine stitch. Stitch velcro strip to front of bib and to skirt waistband.
Attach skirt to bib with velcro.

Stacked cable

Stacked cable

Stem/outline

Smocked sundress

This pretty sundress is a project any beginner stitcher can make successfully and easily. It requires very little sewing ability; there are only two side seams, two hems, and four ribbon straps. It is an ideal project for the summer.

Materials

cotton or cotton polyester fabric (see below for advice on measurements)
satin ribbon—1.5 m (1½ yd)
embroidery cotton—4 skeins
1 dot transfer sheet for hand pleating

Cutting instructions

Cut two lengths of fabric, measuring from underarm to knee or calf, adding 6 cm (2¼ in) for hems. In France, sundresses are hemmed at the calf rather than at the knee, which gives a more romantic look, particularly for little girls.

Pleating and stitch instructions

Machine stitch narrow top hem on front and back sections.
Pleat ten rows front and back, directly underneath top hem.
Prepare and divide pleats.
The stitches used in this project are: *cable, baby wave,* and *trellis.*
Follow stitch diagram to smock.

Finishing

Remove all gathering threads.
Block.
Press open seam allowances.
With right sides together, matching up smocking, pin front to back at sides.
Stitch along seam line.
Cut ribbon into four. Pin two pieces to front and back. Stitch in place, tie with bow, and tack bow in place.
Slip stitch bottom hem.

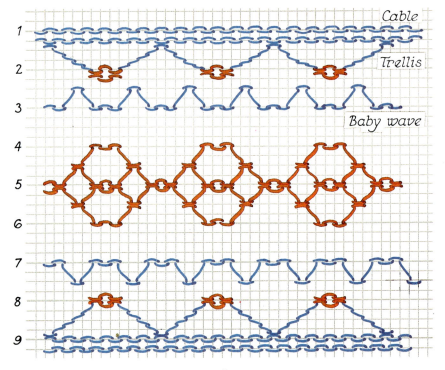

Smocked party dress

This book would be incomplete without at least one party dress for a little girl. This dress was designed with Christmas in mind. But the geometric pattern will adapt to any colour scheme and occasion.

Materials

commercial pattern, age 3–6 years
suggested fabrics—wool, cotton and wool
  blend, cotton poplins
embroidery cotton—2 colour design
1 narrow ribbon
2 dot transfer sheets for hand pleating
notions—according to pattern

Pleating and stitch instructions

Pleat the number of rows needed for the design, which goes from shoulder to waist. Prepare and divide pleats.
The stitches used for this project are: *cable, trellis, baby wave, chain, french knot,* and *bouillon knot.*
Follow stitch diagram to smock, adapting top flower pattern to the size. The last row of smocking should fall at waist level.

Finishing

Remove all gathering threads. Block. Weave ribbon in place and tack on bows.

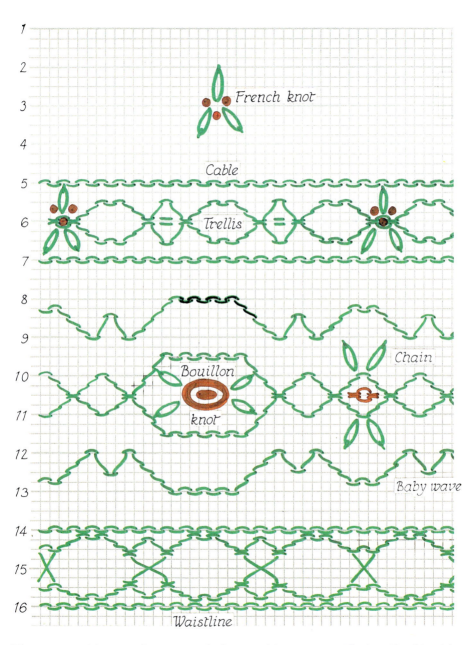

French knot

Cable

Trellis

Chain

Bouillon
knot

Baby wave

Waistline

Place commercial pattern front on smocked piece, mark pattern with tailor's chalk. Along pattern outline, machine stitch smocking to prevent fraying. Do this with a small stitch setting.

Now follow directions given in pattern.

Smocked Easter egg

Here is an idea for a smocked Easter egg – one that will not melt and could last forever.

The project involves 'picture smocking' as for the mobile and the making up is similar.

Materials

a polystyrene egg
fabric—three times diameter of egg, cut to exact height of egg
embroidery cotton—5 colour design
1 dot transfer sheet for hand pleating

Pleating and stitch instructions

This egg measured 22 cm ($8\frac{1}{4}$ in) high and 35 cm ($13\frac{1}{4}$ in) wide. The strip of plain poplin measured 22 × 90 cm ($8\frac{1}{4}$ × 35 in). Pleat twenty-one rows. Prepare and divide pleats.

The stitches used for this project are: *cable, stem, trellis, full wave, crossed diamond, stacked cables, chain, double flowerette, french knot*, and *whipped spider web*.

Follow stitch diagram to smock.

N.B. This project is for an advanced level. Leave first and last gathering thread unsmocked.

Finishing

Follow the same finishing directions as for the smocked mobile, except for the rosette ribbon and fitting the crossbars.

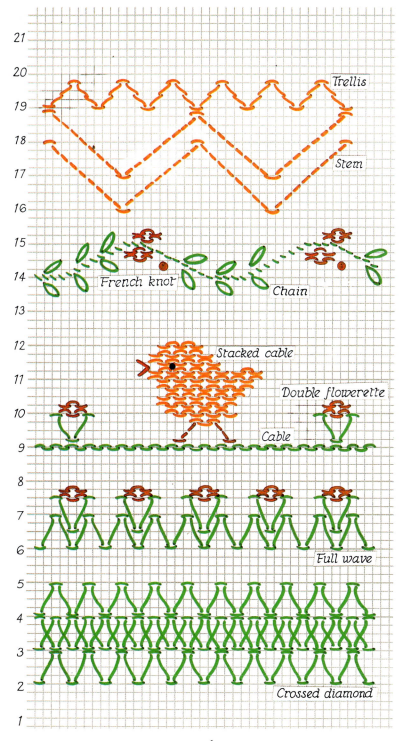

Trellis

Stem

French knot

Chain

Stacked cable

Double flowerette

Cable

Full wave

Crossed diamond

Supply sources

Fine cotton and cotton and wool blends, cotton crêpe:
Clert & Bonnassieux
B.P. 50
69170 Tarare
France

Embroidery cotton and pearl cotton:
Dollfus Mieg & Cie.
50 bld. Sebastapol
Paris 75003
France

Pleating machine:
Read Pleaters
P.O. Box 584
Bergvlei, 2012
South Africa

Dot transfer sheets:
Deighton's
Barnstaple
Devon
England

The above addresses are manufacturers; write to them to find the nearest retailer in your area.

Acknowledgements

I would like to give special thanks to the following friends for their support in writing this book.

Without the girls at Needleworks, in New Orleans, I could not have written any books on needlecraft. They have unselfishly taught me everything, and they have kept me informed on all new trends and techniques that have evolved in the United States.

I would like to give recognition to two talented smocking designers, Ellen McCarn and Mollie Jane Taylor. Their designs opened up new horizons for us. What artist or designer is not inspired by another's work.

Thanks to Françoise Grosgogeat, the projects in this book were made up with a professional's touch.

Last but not least, a grateful thank you to Ruth Levy and Elizabeth O'Connor for checking my text.